Exploring Science

The Exploring Science series is designed to familiarize young students with science topics taught in grades 4–9. The topics in each book are divided into knowledge and understanding sections, followed by exploration by means of simple projects or experiments. The topics are also sequenced from easiest to more complex, and should be worked through until the correct level of attainment for the age and ability of the student is reached. Carefully planned Test Yourself questions at the end of each topic allow the student to gain a sense of achievement on mastering the subject.

EXPLORING
SOIL AND ROCKS

Ed Catherall

STECK-VAUGHN
LIBRARY
Austin, Texas

Exploring Science

Electricity
Energy Sources
Light
Magnets
Soil and Rocks
Sound
Uses of Energy
Weather

Cover illustrations:
Above left A water buffalo is used to cultivate a rice field in
China.
Above right Diagram of rock strata, showing movement along a
fault.
Below Rock formation in Monument Valley, Utah.

Frontispiece Deposits of weathered and eroded rock and soil
have been turned into fertile farmland in this mountain valley in
Kashmir, India.

Editor: Elizabeth Spiers/Cally Chambers
Editor, American Edition: Susan Wilson
Series Designer: Ross George

**Published in the United States in 1991 by Steck-Vaughn Co.,
Austin, Texas,** a subsidiary of National Education Corporation.

First published in 1990 by
Wayland (Publishers) Ltd.

Library of Congress Cataloging-in-Publication Data

Catherall, Ed.
  Exploring soil and rocks / Ed Catherall.

    p.   cm.—(Exploring science)
    Includes bibliography references (p.) and index.
    Summary: Discusses soil composition and earth's geology. Includes
activities and experiments.
    ISBN 0-8114-2595-9
    1. Geology—Juvenile literature.   2. Geology—Experiments—
Juvenile literature.   3. Soils—Juvenile literature.   4. Soils—
Experiments—Juvenile literature.   [1. Geology.   2. Soils.]
I. Title.   II. Series: Catherall, Ed. Exploring science.
QE29.C375   1991   90-10024
550—dc20   CIP
                                                  AC

Typeset by Multifacit Graphics, Keyport, NJ
Printed in Italy by G. Canale C.S.p.A., Turin
Bound in the United States by Lake Book Manufacturing Inc., Melrose Park, IL
    2 3 4 5 6 7 8 9 0 Ca 95 94 93 92

Contents

WHAT IS SOIL?

Soil is a complex material that is derived from the broken down bedrock which lies below it. It is composed of clay, mineral grains, rock fragments, and decomposed plant and animal material.

Soil is the home of many living organisms which can be as large as rabbits or as small as bacteria. They all help to break down the soil to provide valuable nutrients for living plants. One handful of soil can contain over 1.5 billion bacteria, which live in the spaces between the soil particles. Water can also occupy these tiny air spaces and is important in maintaining life in and around the soil. Without soil and water, plants would not be able to grow and convert energy from the sun into food for people and animals.

Soils are identified by their color and texture. The color is due to the amount of iron and kinds of minerals present. The texture depends on the size of the particles that make up the soil. In soil analysis, the sizes used to describe soil types are: gravel; coarse sand; fine sand; silt; and clay.

To get an idea of the grain size, rub some soil between your fingers. Gravel soils are full of small stones and pebbles. All sandy soils feel gritty, but coarse sand is grittier than fine sand. Silt soils are only slightly rough. Clay soils feel smooth when dry, but sticky when wet.

All over the world people use soil to grow plants for food. This country school in Japan has a vegetable garden.

ACTIVITY

YOUR LOCAL SOIL

YOU NEED

- **some local soil**
- **a scale or balance**
- **newspaper**
- **a magnifying glass**
- **plastic bags or tubs**
- **a wide-mesh sieve**
- **a fine-mesh sieve or strainer**

1 Weigh your soil sample.
2 Open a newspaper on the floor and tip your soil sample onto it.
3 Spread out the soil and break up any lumps.

4 Look at the soil through the magnifying glass. Pick out any live animals and put them in containers. Are there any animal remains?
5 Pick out any plant material you see.

6 Tip all the soil onto a wide-mesh sieve. Shake the soil through the sieve onto newspaper. Stones and large particles will stay in the sieve. This is coarse soil. Weigh it.

7 Put the soil on the newspaper through the fine-mesh sieve onto another piece of newspaper. The soil that remains on the fine-mesh sieve is medium soil. The soil that passes through the sieve is fine soil. Weigh both soils.
8 Make a bar graph to show the amount of coarse, medium, and fine soil in your sample.

 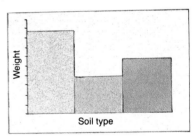

9 What color is the fine soil?
10 Mix a little water with the fine soil.
11 Feel the fine soil and try to identify it, using the information on page 6.

TEST YOURSELF

1. What does soil consist of?
2. Describe how you would identify fine soil particles.
3. Why is soil important to people?

SOIL PROFILES

This soil profile was dug in North Yorkshire, England.

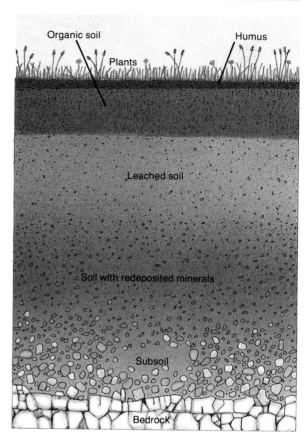

Organic soil
Humus
Plants
Leached soil
Soil with redeposited minerals
Subsoil
Bedrock

Soil profiles are not always the same but it is possible to identify certain layers.

A soil profile is a cross section through soil. If you dig a hole down to bedrock, you will see a soil profile. You might even be able to see layers called soil horizons.

The five main horizons found in soil profiles are given the letters: O, A, B, C, and R. O is the horizon where dead leaves collect. In the A horizon, minerals are dissolved by seeping water, a process called leaching. They are carried down into the B horizon. The C horizon consists of the weathered bedrock and the R horizon is the unweathered bedrock. Not all these horizons are present in simple soils, but in complex soils each horizon may be divided further into two or more zones.

There are six main soil types. They are identified according to the different climates of the world. Tundra soils form in wet areas where the subsoil is permanently frozen. Podzols are the light soils of temperate forests. Latosols are the red soils of hot, wet tropical and subtropical forests. Prairie soils occur between wet and dry regions. Chestnuts and chernozems are the brown to black soils of partly arid (dry) grasslands and forests. Light-colored desert soils form in the driest regions.

ACTIVITY

DIGGING A SOIL PROFILE

YOU NEED

- **a spade**
- **a newspaper**
- **a magnifying glass**
- **a ruler**
- **a 3-ft length of wood**
- **liquid glue (not superglue)**
- **a spatula to spread the glue**

WARNING: This is hard work. Get an adult to help you.

1 Choose an area of undisturbed ground away from trees and dig a hole in the soil.
2 Look at the soil and measure how far the plant roots go down into it.
3 Break up the soil on the newspaper. With your magnifying glass, examine animal and plant remains. Can you identify them?

4 Dig down as far as you can. Make the hole large enough to see the sides. Make the sides vertical.
5 Use a ruler to measure the thickness of the layers. Identify them.
6 Mark the layer depth on the wood.
7 Coat one surface of the wood with a thick layer of glue.
8 Scatter the soils from each layer in the correct place on your wood. Leave the wood until the glue sets. You have made a record, called a soil monolith, of the soil profile.

9 Make different records of different holes. Compare them.

WARNING: Be careful not to inhale the fumes from the glue.

TEST YOURSELF

1. What is a soil profile?
2. Draw an example of a soil profile and label the layers.
3. Describe how you would make a soil monolith.

THE ACIDITY OF SOIL

There are many factors and chemical reactions that influence how acidic a soil is.

Bacteria and fungi in the soil cause dead plants and animals to decompose. This decaying material (humus) is broken down to carbon dioxide gas, which is weakly acidic when dissolved in water. Even when they are living, all the organisms in the soil are releasing carbon dioxide as they breathe. The acidity from both these sources helps to break the soil down to nutrients that plants use for growth.

When rain falls it dissolves carbon dioxide from the atmosphere and becomes slightly acidic. This acidity is increased if the rain falls through gases from industrial pollution. So even before water reaches the soil it is acidic.

Soil acidity will vary according to where in the soil profile a sample is taken. It may be more acidic in the layer of humus than in a horizon farther down. It will also depend on the type of bedrock that the soil has come from.

Soil acidity can be measured with scientific instruments or color indicators. It can be compared on a scale of pH numbers. The lower the pH number (below 7), the more acid the soil is. A pH number of 7 is neutral, and a pH above 7 is alkaline.

Plants can grow among decaying leaf litter. Growth and decay both make the soil acidic.

ACTIVITY

YOU NEED

- **2 large red cabbage leaves**
- **a bowl**
- **a wooden spoon**
- **hot or boiling water**
- **2 glass jars**
- **white vinegar**
- **a teaspoon**
- **soil samples**

WARNING: Be careful when using hot water. Get an adult to help you.

1 Tear the red cabbage leaves into pieces and put them in the bowl.
2 Cover the leaves with very hot water. Use the wooden spoon to squeeze the juice from the leaves.

3 Let the cabbage stand in the water for one hour.
4 Put some of the purple cabbage water into each jar.

5 Add vinegar to one jar, a drop at a time, until the water turns deep red.
6 Add one spoonful of soil to each jar.

7 Put lids on the jars and shake them. If the purple water turns red, your soil is acid. If the red water turns purple, your soil is alkaline. If the water does not change color in either jar, your soil is neutral.

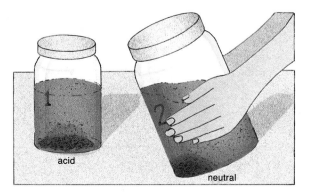

acid

neutral

8 Test a range of different soils.

Remember: if you test the top (humus) layer of soil, it will usually be acidic. Dig down to get a better sample.

TEST YOURSELF

1. What makes rain acidic?
2. Why is the decayed layer (humus), likely to be more acidic?
3. How can acidity be measured?

THE SOIL AND ITS PLANTS

Plants have adapted, over thousands of years, to grow in a wide range of habitats.

Left Grasses and reeds thrive in this watery marshland in Norfolk, England.

Below Palm trees can survive in parts of the hot, dry Sahara desert in northern Africa.

There are thousands of different kinds of plants, and each kind has particular needs and will thrive only in suitable conditions. These conditions can be divided into physical factors and biotic (living) factors. The physical factors include the amount of water available, the amount of light, the temperature, air movements (whether the plant is exposed or sheltered), the terrain (mountains and valleys), and type of soil.

The amount of water that each plant needs is varied. Some live in water. Others live in marshes and need a lot of water. Most plants need a reasonable amount of water, but desert plants need hardly any. All green plants need some light. Some plants can withstand the glaring sunlight of the tropics, while others live on the floors of dark forests. Plants grow in all parts of the world, in temperatures ranging from hot desert to the cold of the polar regions. Some plants live deep in valleys, while others live on the tops of mountains.

The soil type, acidity, and texture are very important. Some plants, like heather, have adapted to sandy, humus-rich acidic soils. Roses will thrive on slightly alkaline clay soils. Orchids prefer the more alkaline soils that lie over chalk. In fact, for any soil type, some plants will have become adapted to the conditions.

The biotic, or living, factors affecting a plant include all the neighboring plants, all the animals that live off the plant, and often, the influence of humans.

ACTIVITY

GROWING PLANTS IN DIFFERENT SOILS

YOU NEED

- **an area where plants can grow undisturbed**
- **a spade**
- **a garden fork**
- **builder's sand**
- **a bag of lime**
- **materials as for tests on page 11**
- **a rake**
- **a book about wild plants**

WARNING: Be careful when using lime. Do not get it on your hands.

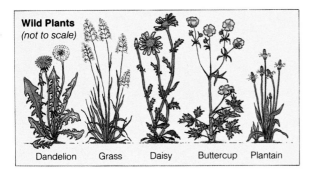

Wild Plants
(not to scale)

Dandelion   Grass   Daisy   Buttercup   Plantain

1 What is the soil like in your area? Which weeds grow on this soil?
2 Remove all the plants from two 3-foot-square areas of soil.
3 Turn the soil over with the spade and remove the remains of roots.

4 Mix builder's sand with one area of soil. Take a sample to test acidity.
5 Mix lime into the soil in another 3-foot-square area. Take a sample to test for alkalinity.

6 Rake both surfaces.
7 Record all the weeds that grow in each type of soil. Which weeds are found in both types of soil? Which weeds grow in only one? Does one type soil have more weeds?

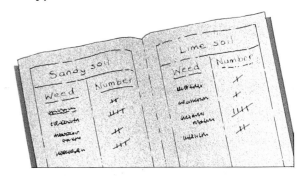

TEST YOURSELF

1. Describe four physical factors that influence plant growth.
2. In what way does soil influence plant growth?
3. What are the biotic factors that influence plant growth?

ORGANIC AND INORGANIC SOILS

The organic material in soil is formed by plants and animals that live in the topsoil. Soils can be called "organic" or "inorganic" but the only true kind of organic soil is peat. This is because peat is made only from plant material (see page 16). Peat can be very thick because layers of dead plants build up faster than they decay.

Other soils contain inorganic as well as organic material. The inorganic content is the nonliving rock fragments and mineral grains made from the broken bedrock. A soil with a high inorganic content may not be very fertile for plant growth. But it becomes richer as more plants and small organisms live and decay in it.

Certain vegetables, called legumes, have nodules (small swellings) in their roots. Bacteria live in these nodules, making nitrogen gas from the air into nitrogen com-

Legumes have root nodules containing bacteria that convert nitrogen in the air to nitrogen compounds that the plant can use.

pounds that the plant uses to form plant proteins. These proteins are the "building blocks" for growth. When legumes die, other bacteria live in the dead remains, making them decay, or decompose. These bacteria break down the plant proteins to ammonia and other nitrates, which go into the soil. Other plants absorb the nitrates, to form their own plant proteins. These plants grow and die and the bacteria break them down to form ammonia and nitrates again. In this way the cycle continues.

When roots, stems, and leaves decay below the surface, humus is formed. Humus is a dark substance, rich in minerals and nutrients essential for plant growth.

ACTIVITY

YOU NEED

- **3 large glass jars with lids**
- **a bag of sand**
- **garden soil and potting compost**
- **water**
- **a magnifying glass**

1 Put the sand in one jar, the garden soil in another, and the potting soil in the third.

2 Put the same amount in each jar, until the jars are half full.

3 Fill the jars with water. Put on lids.

4 Shake the jars. Let them stand. Watch the particles settle.

5 Where are the largest particles? How many layers can you see?

6 Draw each jar, showing the different layers.

7 Look at any stuff floating with the magnifying glass. It is made of decayed plants, or organic material.

8 Compare the amount of organic material in each jar. Which has the most? This is the best organic soil.

9 Does your garden soil have a high or low organic content?

10 Test other soils.

TEST YOURSELF

1. What is the difference between inorganic and organic soil?
2. Bacteria are found in the nodules on the roots of vegetable plants called legumes. What do these bacteria do?
3. Explain the process of plant decay. Why is it called a cycle?

FOSSIL FUELS

The fossil fuels are peat, coal, oil, and natural gas (methane). Besides being fuels, coal and oil are used to make medicines, dyes, and plastics. In freshwater marshes and river deltas in warm climates, plants grow rapidly. When they die, they are quickly covered by mud and silt. Once covered, there is no air for the usual decay bacteria to survive (see page 14). Special bacteria, that can live without air, decay the material slowly into hydrocarbons (chemicals containing only carbon and hydrogen).

The mud and silt continue to pile up on top of the decayed material, forcing it deeper and squashing it. First, the plant material becomes peat. Then, as it is forced even deeper, it becomes brown coal, which is known as lignite. Gradually, it is forced so deep that all the weight on top presses it into a hard, black substance called coal. Most of our coal layers were living plants 225 million to 345 million years ago.

In shallow seas tiny animals and plants died and sank to the seabed, where they were buried by mud and sand. They were also decomposed by bacteria that could live without air. Gradually, this organic material was pushed deeper and deeper as the mud piled on top.

As time passed the Earth's crust changed (see page 38). The heat and pressure turned the decayed animals and plants into oil. Where pressure and heat were very great, natural gas was formed from the oil.

Peat is hand dug for fuel in the Isle of Skye, Scotland (left). A machine can work on a larger scale in a coal mine (right).

ACTIVITY

1 Look in the atlas. Where is the coalfield nearest you? Where is the nearest oilfield?

2 Find the major oilfields of the world.
3 Find out how oil and gas are drilled, transported to the refineries, and eventually reach us, in different forms. How do we use oil and gas?
4 Search the newspapers for details of oil disasters, such as spillage or rig fires. Write your own reports.
5 Look at pieces of coal with a magnifying glass. Can you see any evidence of plant material in the coal?
6 What is coal used for? How is it mined? Find out all you can about coal production and distribution

Oil platforms sometimes have to burn off the natural gas that is found with oil deposits.

TEST YOURSELF

1. What can coal and oil be used for if they are not used as fuels?
2. How was coal made?
3. How were oil and gas made?

THE HISTORY OF THE EARTH

Sometimes when plants and animals died they did not completely decay. Most of the soft parts decayed, leaving shells or bones, and less often, the woody parts of plants. Over a long time these leftover structures turned to stone and became fossils. Imprints left by animals and plants also became fossils. Fossils are examined to find out their age and to tell us more about Earth's history and past life forms.

Geologists estimate that our planet is about 4.6 billion years old, and its time can be divided into four main time zones or eras. The first era lasted from 4.6 billion to 570 million years ago. It is called the Pre-Cambrian era, and we know little about life at that time. Because most creatures had soft bodies that would have decayed easily, the rocks contain few fossils. Also, pressure from the rocks of later eras crushed the fossils there might have been.

The next era is the ancient life, or Paleozoic, era, from 570 million to 225 million years ago. Rocks from this era are rich in fossils. Most are sea creatures, including early fish. There are also some plant fossils.

The next era is the middle life, or Mesozoic, era. This lasted from 225 million to 65 million years ago. This was the age of reptiles, including the dinosaurs.

The last era is the new life, or Cenozoic, era, from 65 million years ago until today. This is the age of mammals and the plants that we know today. The first humans were very recent; only about 2 to 5 million years ago. This is only a very short time when you think of the age of the Earth.

Right *Fossils indicate past forms of life in the Earth's history. Geological time is divided into eras, periods, and epochs.*

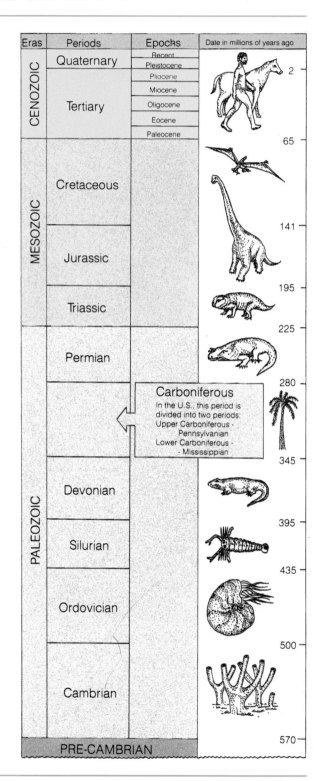

Eras	Periods	Epochs	Date in millions of years ago
CENOZOIC	Quaternary	Recent	
		Pleistocene	2
	Tertiary	Pliocene	
		Miocene	
		Oligocene	
		Eocene	
		Paleocene	65
MESOZOIC	Cretaceous		
			141
	Jurassic		
			195
	Triassic		225
PALEOZOIC	Permian		
			280
	Carboniferous — In the U.S., this period is divided into two periods: Upper Carboniferous - Pennsylvanian Lower Carboniferous - Mississippian		
			345
	Devonian		
			395
	Silurian		
			435
	Ordovician		
			500
	Cambrian		
			570
PRE-CAMBRIAN			

ACTIVITY

MAKING A MODEL FOSSIL

YOU NEED

- **a collection of fossils**
- **a plastic carton and pan**
- **plaster of Paris**
- **scissors**
- **a spoon**
- **petroleum jelly**
- **a seashell**

1 Look at the fossil collection. Which are actual fossils and which are fossil imprints?
2 Half fill the plastic pan with water.
3 Stir in plaster of Paris, until it is like a thick cream.
4 Pour the plaster into the carton.
5 Cover the shell with petroleum jelly. Wait for the plaster to just harden and then press the shell into the plaster without burying it.

6 Let the plaster set.
7 Carefully lift out your shell. You have made a fossil imprint.
8 Cover this fossil imprint with petroleum jelly.

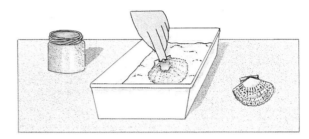

9 Make more creamy plaster.
10 Pour it into the fossil imprint.
11 Wait for the plaster to set, then lift out your plaster fossil from its plaster mold.

Below *This is a fossil of a sea lily. It was once a living animal.*

TEST YOURSELF

1. How old do geologists think that our planet is?
2. What are the four main geological eras?
3. When did mammals appear on Earth?

MOVEMENT OF THE EARTH'S PLATES

Our planet consists of a series of layers. The outer layer, called the crust, is the layer on which we live. It is only 10 mi. thick under the oceans, although up to 25 mi. thick under the land. This solid crust covers a part-liquid, part-solid mantle that is 1,700 mi. thick. The mantle covers the core, which can be divided into two parts. The outer core, which is probably molten (melted) rock, is 2,000 mi. thick. The inner core is very dense and probably solid. It is about 750 mi. thick. Rocks get denser and heavier from surface to core, so the crust contains the lightest materials, while the inner core is four to five times denser.

The Earth's crust is like a cracked egg-shell. The cracks lead down to the mantle. The pieces of "eggshell" are the Earth's plates, on which the continents ride. Molten mantle material, called magma, oozes up through the cracks. It becomes solid and forms new plate material. This forces the plates apart.

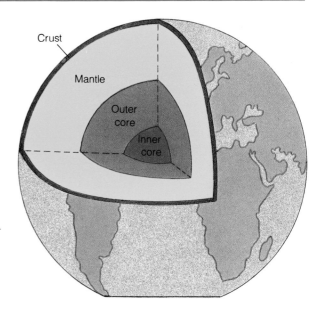

Above *The Earth in cross section.*

Below *The plates that make up the Earth's crust are forced apart where molten magma rises to the surface, causing plates to push up against each other or one to be pushed under another in a subduction zone.*

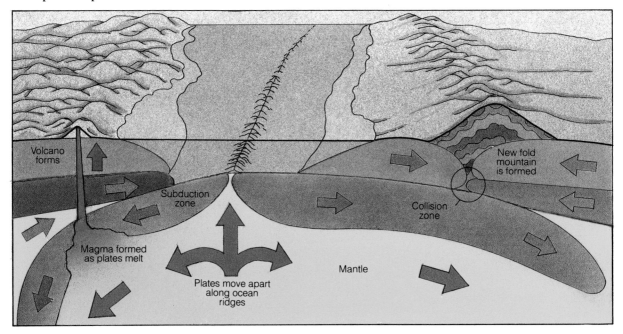

The plates ride on convection currents caused by the heat of the mantle. As the plates move, they push and pull against each other. One plate may be forced under another plate, to become part of the mantle again. Sometimes, the plates meet and buckle up, making mountains. This plate movement is called continental drift.

It is thought that 200 million years ago the Earth consisted of just one continent called Pangaea. This cracked, and the pieces drifted apart. The pieces were in different positions 60 million years ago from their positions today. The pieces still move; perhaps in another 60 million years, the Earth will look different again.

ACTIVITY

YOU NEED

- **maps showing continental drift**
- **an atlas**
- **tracing paper**

1 Look at maps showing continental drift. What happened to India?
2 Look at an atlas. Use two separate sheets of tracing paper to draw outlines of South America and Africa.

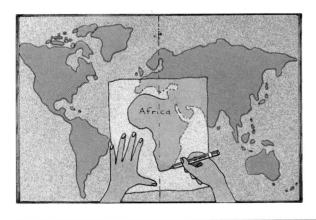

3 Fit these two outlines together. This is how we think they were when they were part of Pangaea.

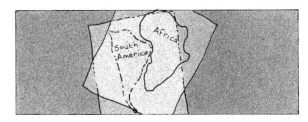

4 Trace the east coast of North America and the west coast of Europe. Try to fit these together, as they could have been in Pangaea.

5 Try to find out how other continents fit together as Pangaea.

TEST YOURSELF

1. Name the layers that make up our planet.
2. In a cross section through the Earth, where would you expect to find the densest material? Why?
3. What is continental drift?

VOLCANOES AND EARTHQUAKES

Volcanoes occur in three kinds of area: where new plate is formed along constructive plate boundaries; where old plate is destroyed along destructive plate boundaries; and where a plate slides over a thin area in the Earth's crust called a hot spot.

The volcanoes found at constructive plate boundaries and hot spots are rarely explosive. The magma that comes to the surface is smooth and fluid, and so the eruptions are mild and effusive.

The magma at destructive plate boundaries is molten plate material and is lumpy and thick. This makes it difficult for the volcanic gases to escape. They build up until they are released in a violent explosion that can be very dangerous.

Earthquakes occur where the Earth's plates move past each other. Sometimes

A fountain of lava is thrown out of Kilauea, Hawaii. Great destruction can occur as molten lava sets fire to trees, or whole towns, before cooling and solidifying.

the plates do not slide smoothly and they get jammed. Pressure builds up until eventually the rocks break. The plates then move suddenly, causing the ground to shake in an earthquake. This happens along the San Andreas fault in California, where the Pacific plate is sliding north past the North American plate.

Earthquakes can cause damage to buildings and roads, and loss of life. So scientists try to predict them by monitoring the movement of plates. Earthquakes' strengths are measured on the Richter scale.

ACTIVITY

VOLCANOES

YOU NEED

- **a video of a volcano erupting**
- **a video recorder and monitor**
- **an atlas**

1 Watch a video of a volcano erupting. Most videos show hot-spot volcanoes, as these are easier to film. Notice the molten lava.
2 Look for the position of famous volcanoes in an atlas. Use your library to find out more about volcanoes.
3 Because of movements of the plates, volcanoes have occurred in different places. Often, only the center, or crater, of a volcano is left. Where is the volcano nearest you?

EARTHQUAKES

YOU NEED

- **newspaper reports of earthquakes**

1 Read the account of an earthquake.
2 What was the tremor's strength, as measured on the Richter scale?
3 How much devastation (damage) was caused? Was there loss of life?
4 Where was the center of the earthquake? Which of the Earth's plates were involved?
5 Has an earthquake happened before in the same area?
6 Was there any advance warning and, if so, what steps were taken?
7 Write a report about it.

Right *This portable seismometer records on a graph the tremors caused by an earthquake.*

TEST YOURSELF

1. Where do volcanoes occur?
2. Explain why some volcanoes erupt with explosive force.
3. What causes earthquakes?

HOW MOUNTAINS ARE FORMED

There are four main types of mountain: fold mountains, volcanoes, block mountains, and dome mountains. Mountain ranges may take millions of years to form.

Fold mountains are found in the middle of continents, along ancient plate boundaries. They are made from sedimentary rocks once deposited on ocean floors, and later compressed, folded, and forced up. About 50 million years ago, the Indian and Asian plates buckled the ocean sediment between them to make the Himalayas.

Where plates collide in a coastal region, volcanic mountain ranges form. These are made up of volcanoes, with smaller amounts of folded sediments strung between them. The Coast Ranges of North America were made in this way.

Block mountains are found where a piece of land has been slowly lifted between two long faults. Two blocks may be raised next to each other and the land between sinks, creating a rift valley. The Vosges and Black Forest blocks in Europe stand on either side of the Rhine River rift valley.

Dome mountains are made in different ways. Sedimentary rocks can be folded and shaped into a dome, or magma may be forced up beneath them, pushing them into a dome. Sometimes these rocks may be worn away and the dome of solidified magma is exposed.

The Black Hills of South Dakota are examples of dome mountains. The dome is solidified magma that has become exposed.

ACTIVITY

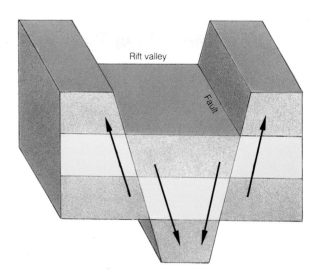

Rift valley

Fault

1 Place the 5 handkerchiefs on top of each other on a smooth surface. They represent 5 rock layers.
2 Place a book at either end of the pile of handkerchiefs. Each book is a plate in the Earth's crust.
3 Slowly slide the books toward each other. Notice how the handkerchiefs fold. The upside of a fold is the anticline; the downside is the syncline.

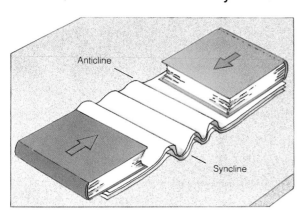

Anticline

Syncline

4 Look in your atlas. Find the fold mountains of the Himalayas, the Alps, the Rockies, and the Andes. Look at a map of the Earth's plates. How were these mountains formed?

5 Look in your atlas for the East African rift valley. Look at the northern end of this rift valley. Notice how the sea could rush in and flood this valley, if the rift gets any larger.

Below Snow highlights the folds in the Himalayan mountain peaks, India.

TEST YOURSELF

1. Name the four main kinds of mountains?
2. How do block mountains and rift valleys form?
3. How do fold mountains like the Himalayas form?

METEORITES AND IMPACT CRATERS

The surface of the moon has many craters. Some were formed by erupting volcanoes, but most were made by meteorites that fell from space.

On a clear night you can sometimes see meteor trails in the sky. They are called shooting stars. Some small planets in our solar system broke up a long time ago, and these pieces travel around the sun, just as the Earth does. If some of these pieces come near enough to the Earth, they enter our atmosphere (air surrounding Earth).

The meteor is heated up as it passes through the air, causing it to glow. The oxygen in the air will also make it burn up, creating the meteor trails that you see. Most meteors, therefore, never reach the surface of the Earth.

When a meteor does hit the Earth's surface, it is called a meteorite. If the meteorite is large, it creates an impact crater when it strikes the surface, like one crater formed in Arizona.

The moon has no atmosphere, so meteors that approach it cannot burn up. This is why the moon has many impact craters.

Meteorites that strike the Earth's surface can be analyzed and roughly dated. They are of two main types: stony ones that are similar to the Earth's crust and mantle, and heavy ones that are similar to the Earth's core. These contain a lot of iron.

ACTIVITY

YOU NEED

- **a large stone**
- **an area of soft, dry sand**
- **an atlas of the moon**
- **binoculars**

1 Drop a large stone onto soft sand.
2 Look at the crater caused by the stone. Notice how the sand forms a raised area around the rim.

3 How could you make a larger crater in the sand?
4 Look at the atlas of the moon. Many of the craters are the centers of volcanoes, but some of the craters were caused by meteorites.
5 On a clear night, look at the full moon through binoculars. Compare the craters that you can see with those on the map.
6 On your next visit to a museum, look at the meteorites. What are they made of? Where did they fall?

A Geminid meteor (the long streak on the far left) was photographed from California in 1980. The smaller streaks are stars.

TEST YOURSELF

1. Where do meteors and meteorites come from?
2. What is a meteor trail?
3. Why are there so many impact craters on the moon?

IGNEOUS ROCKS

Igneous rocks are made from molten material that has cooled and solidified. The word igneous comes from the Latin *ignis*, meaning fire.

Molten magma from beneath the Earth's crust rises toward the surface. If it reaches the surface through volcanoes and vents, it is called lava. The lava cools and solidifies to become volcanic or extrusive rock. Where the magma does not quite reach the surface, it cools very slowly underground and becomes an intrusive rock.

Below ground, magma cools very slowly and intrusive rocks like granite develop large crystals. At the surface, lava loses its heat so quickly that it solidifies before large crystals can form. Some lava cools so quickly that it produces a dark glass called obsidian. Others cool rapidly enough so that cracks from shrinkage, called joints, form. These may produce strange shapes in the new rock.

The thick magma that is thrown out of explosive volcanoes (see page 22) is full of trapped air bubbles. This frothy magma solidifies into pumice, which is very light. Volcanoes also throw ashes and dust into the air. In time, pieces of ash become compacted and form a rock called tuff.

When joints in cooled lava are close together, they produce column shapes like the stepping stones of the Giant's Causeway, Ireland.

ACTIVITY

YOU NEED

- **a collection of igneous rocks, including pumice stone and granite**
- **a magnifying glass**
- **a copper coin**
- **a steel nail**
- **a basin of warm water**

1 Look at your collection of igneous rocks through the magnifying glass. Can you identify them?
2 Look at a piece of granite. Notice that it is a coarse-grained rock.
3 Look at the granite through the magnifying glass. Can you see quartz crystals in it? You may also see crystals of feldspar and mica.
4 Scratch the granite with your finger nail, a copper coin, and the nail. Can you make a mark in it?

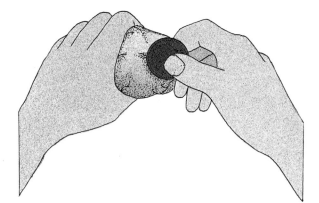

5 Hold the piece of pumice. Notice how light it feels. Place the pumice in a basin of warm water. Notice how the stone floats.

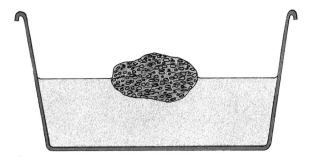

6 Hold the stone under water. What do you see coming from the stone? Where did this come from?

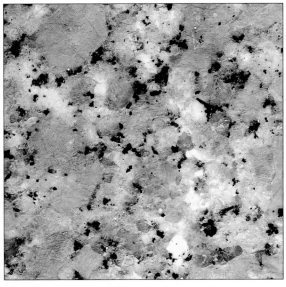

Above *A cross section of granite shows crystals of feldspar (pink), mica (black), and quartz (white).*

TEST YOURSELF

1. What are igneous rocks made from?
2. Name four different kinds of igneous rock.
3. Why is pumice so light?

ICE EROSION

Snow falls on high mountains and builds up in hollows. Most of the snow becomes compacted into ice that builds up and begins to move downhill. New ice is continually being made and adds to the very slow river of ice, or glacier, that makes its path down the mountain.

When water freezes, it expands. This happens in the rock around the glacier. The expansion splits the rock apart and as the glacier moves, it collects the debris, as well as pulling material from the solid rock beneath. The rock collected by the glacier in this way is called moraine. The moraine itself then acts to grind away still more rock in the glacier's path. In time, a U-shaped valley is eroded as mountain rock is

You can see the surface moraine in this picture of the Baltoro Glacier in Pakistan.

carried down toward the lowlands.

Lower down the mountain the air is warmer and the glacier melts. At the glacier's end, or snout, water flows away, carrying the finer moraine with it. This is deposited on the land below as glacial till.

When the world's climate cools, the polar icecaps grow very large and an ice age results. In these periods, glaciation and erosion (see page 34) by ice is widespread. Earth has had many ice ages, but the last ended around 11,000 years ago. Even in today's warmer climate, ice plays a major part in the erosion of mountains.

ACTIVITY

ICE EXPANDS

YOU NEED

- **an ice tray**
- **water**
- **a crayon**
- **a freezer**
- **a screw-top plastic bottle**
- **a plastic bag**
- **a rubber band**

1 Fill the ice tray with water. Notice that the surface of the water is flat.

2 Mark the water level with a crayon.

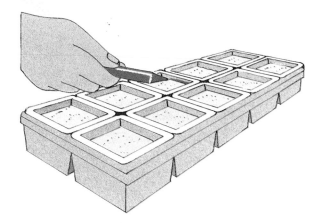

3 Put the ice tray in the freezer.

4 Look at the surface when the water is frozen. Is the ice surface flat? Does the ice take up more or less space than the water did?

5 Fill a plastic bottle with water and screw the lid on.

6 Put it inside a plastic bag and seal with a rubber band.

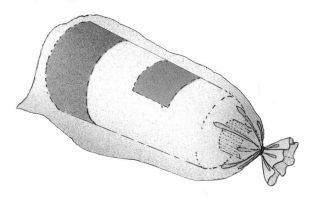

7 Put this bag in the freezer and leave it until the water has completely turned to ice.

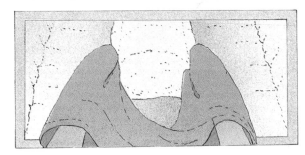

8 What happens to the water?

WARNING: Very cold things from the freezer can hurt your hands; hold them with a dish towel.

TEST YOURSELF

1. Where does the ice in a glacier come from?
2. How does a glacier wear away a U-shaped valley?
3. Where does the moraine in a glacier come from and what happens to it?

WEATHERING

Weathering is the chemical and mechanical breakdown of rocks and minerals. The weathering processes occur to the rock and do not involve material being carried away or eroded (see page 34).

Chemical weathering occurs when a chemical reaction alters the minerals in rock. Rainwater is acidic (see page 10) and, as it soaks into the ground, the acid reacts with certain minerals in the rocks. Calcite in limestone is dissolved by rainwater that flows along its joints (see page 34) and large caverns can be left behind. The acids released by plants and other living organisms can dissolve minerals, too.

Mechanical weathering is due mainly to temperature changes. Water in rock cracks

A scree slope of weathered rock material has formed around this volcanic crater in Iceland. The particles roll down and in time the edges will become less steep.

expands as it freezes and splits the rock apart (see page 30). Ice and frosts can work alone, but often both chemical and mechanical processes occur jointly. In deserts the chemical action caused by infrequent rains and dews breaks down the minerals in the surface layer of rocks. Then, the severe temperature changes between frosty nights and scorching hot days splits away the weak rock. The rocks are weathered in layers and so the process is known as onion-skin weathering.

ACTIVITY

YOU NEED

- **a windy day**
- **a wooden mallet**
- **a few short planks of wood, sharpened at one end**
- **petroleum jelly**
- **a magnifying glass**

WARNING: Get an adult to help you. Using a mallet can be hard work.

1 Look at your house or school. Are there any signs of mechanical weathering on the outside walls? Which side shows the most wear?
2 On a windy day, drive the wood planks into the ground.
3 Put some planks into soil and some in grassy areas.

4 Cover each plank with a layer of petroleum jelly. Wait an hour.

5 Use the magnifying glass to look at each plank. Look for soil particles, sand, or dust sticking to the wood.
6 Which has the most sticking to it?
7 On which side do you find the most soil particles? Why?
8 Carvings on the outside of old churches are often worn away by weathering. Watch for examples.

Gravestones show weathering by lichens which cling to their surface and by rain.

TEST YOURSELF

1. What is weathering?
2. Give examples of both chemical and mechanical weathering.
3. How might mechanical weathering affect the outside of a building?

EROSION

Left *A large stream passage has been worn away by chemical weathering as water flows through cracks in limestone in South Wales.*

Below *The dark color of the Iguacu Waterfalls in northeast Argentina is caused by the soil being carried away in the fast-flowing water.*

Erosion occurs when weathered rocks are carried away. It can be caused by the action of water, wind, ice, animals, and gravity.

Rainwater washes particles of weathered rock and soil into streams and rivers. The force of the downhill flow of a swollen river sweeps away large amounts of rock debris. How much material is eroded depends on its type, but the steeper the slope, the more erosive power a river has. In higher areas near its source, the river erodes material from its channel and cuts a V-shaped valley for itself. As the land flattens, the river flows more slowly. It no longer has the power to erode its channel and has to deposit its load. In this way rivers work to flatten mountains.

The sea has great power to erode coastlines. During storms, waves crash against cliffs, wearing them away and causing cliff falls. Wave action continues to break up

this material along the coastline, until it is deposited as sand along our beaches.

Wind can also have the power to erode. In deserts, winds carry sand and dust near to the ground. This acts like a natural sandblaster and wears away more particles at the base of rocks.

ACTIVITY

1 Line each box with a sheet of plastic. Cut a hole at one end of each box and plastic sheet.
2 Fill one box with sand, and the second box with soil.
3 Half-fill the third box with soil and cover the soil surface with turf.
4 Pack down the turf.

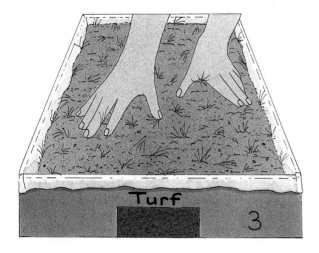

5 Place each box on a slope.
6 Put a jar under the box holes.
7 Using the watering can, water the sand, soil, and turf, near the higher end of each box.
8 Put the same amount of water in each box.

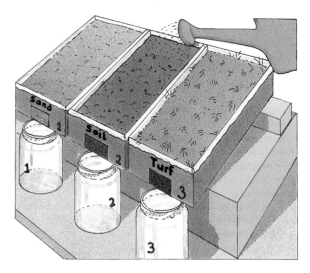

9 Draw what happens to the soil or sand in each of the boxes.
10 How is the sand and soil moved?
11 What happens if water meets a stone on the surface?
12 Look at what is being washed down into the jars.
13 Which box shows the most water erosion? What happens when you increase the slope of each box?
14 Try different kinds of soil.
15 Save the results for page 37.
16 Look for examples of water erosion where you live.

TEST YOURSELF

1. What will eventually happen to all mountains?
2. What is water erosion?
3. How can water and wind cause erosion?

SEDIMENTARY ROCKS

Sedimentary rocks are formed when particles are deposited. There are four stages in their formation.

First, there is weathering, which breaks rocks into small particles (see pages 32 and 34). In the second stage, rock particles are eroded or worn away. This can be done by water, ice, and wind. Water in streams and rivers rolls the rock particles over and over, until bits are chipped off and they become smooth pebbles. These are broken down even further to form sand, mud, clay, or silt. In the third stage, the sand, mud, clay, or silt are deposited on flat plains and in lakes, river estuaries, or the sea, where they become layers of sediment. In the final stage the weight of all these layers of sediment presses down onto the lower layers and turns them into rock.

Water is also trickling through the layers of sediments, depositing dissolved lime, silica (sand), or iron. This holds the grains of sediment together. Lime is formed from the shells and bones of living creatures in the sea. They sink down when they die and become part of the sediment.

Chalk and limestone are sedimentary rocks, consisting almost entirely of the deposited remains of animals. Sandstone is made of sand layers. Conglomerates are made of pebbles. Shale is fine mud. Sedimentary rocks always have strata (layers). Sedimentary rocks will also weather, be transported, be redeposited, and form sedimentary rocks again.

The limestone cliff in Devon, England, is made up of horizontal strata.

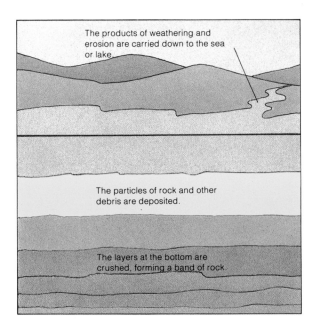

The products of weathering and erosion are carried down to the sea or lake.

The particles of rock and other debris are deposited.

The layers at the bottom are crushed, forming a band of rock.

sand

soil

turfed soil

ACTIVITY

YOU NEED

- **a collection of sedimentary rocks, including chalk, limestone, and shale**
- **a magnifying glass**
- **a jar**
- **white vinegar**

1 Look again at the results of your experiment on page 35. The soil and sand in the trays are pieces of eroded rock. These weathered particles were transported down by the water and deposited as layers of sediment in the jars.

2 Look at your collection of sedimentary rocks. Can you see layers?
3 Can you scratch the rocks with your thumbnail? Notice how soft they are, compared with igneous rocks (see page 29).
4 Put a piece of chalk or limestone in the jar.
5 Cover it with vinegar and notice how it fizzes. This gas is carbon dioxide. Gradually, the chalk will dissolve. This is similar to chemical weathering (see page 32).

TEST YOURSELF

1. What are the four stages in the formation of sedimentary rocks?
2. How is chalk formed?
3. Which is harder—an igneous rock or a sedimentary rock? Why?

METAMORPHIC ROCKS

You know that the Earth's plates are constantly moving. They may collide to form fold-mountain chains, or one plate may be pushed beneath another and the lower plate pushed down into the mantle (see page 20). These plate movements create great pressure and heat. These are so great that they can change the rocks that make up the surface of the plates. These surface rocks can be igneous rocks made from molten magma, or sedimentary rocks deposited by water, ice, or wind.

Molten magma is very hot and heats up surrounding rocks. This source of heat changes the surrounding rocks into metamorphic rocks. Both igneous and sedimentary rocks can be changed into metamor-

Different types of marble are used all over the world to make things as varied as buildings, statues, and table tops. It is popular not only because patterns in the rock are decorative, but also because its hardness makes it difficult to wear away.

phic rocks, but the rock's origin will control what it becomes. If the igneous rock granite is turned into a metamorphic rock, it is called gneiss. Many sedimentary rocks have been turned into metamorphic rocks. The sedimentary rock shale becomes the metamorphic rock slate. Limestone is turned into the metamorphic rock marble. While sedimentary rocks are soft, they harden when transformed into metamorphic rock.

ACTIVITIES

YOU NEED

- **some metamorphic rocks, including slate and marble**
- **a magnifying glass**
- **a jar**
- **white vinegar**
- **a copper coin**
- **a steel nail**

1 Look at your collection of metamorphic rocks through the magnifying glass. Can you identify them?
2 Look at the slate. Notice that it is in layers.
3 Look at the flat surface through the magnifying glass. The particles that originally made the sedimentary rock were fine mud.
4 Look at marble. Record the ways in which it is different from slate.
5 Put a small piece of marble in the jar. Cover it with white vinegar. Does it fizz, as chalk and limestone do?
6 Scratch the metamorphic rocks with the copper coin and the nail. Are they harder than sedimentary ones?

This picture shows pieces of slate. If you look closely you can see its layers.

MAKING A ROCK COLLECTION

YOU NEED

- **a collection of rocks**
- **shallow boxes to hold your rocks**
- **labels**
- **a clear plastic wrapper**

1 Find out about the rocks in your collection.
2 On a label, record where and when the rock was found. Was the rock found above or below the surface?
3 Cover your boxes with clear plastic film to keep dust from your rocks.

TEST YOURSELF

1. Name three kinds of metamorphic rock.
2. How are metamorphic rocks formed?
3. Which types of metamorphic rocks are much harder than the original rock?

MINERALS

Copper deposits in rocks. Copper is usually shiny brown but turns green when it is exposed to air.

A rock can be made up of a number of naturally occurring minerals, of which there are many different kinds. But each mineral consists of only one type of chemical compound. Some compounds are simple, like the calcite of which limestone is composed. Others are very complex, like the feldspars and micas found in granite.

Usually minerals can be classed simply into those that are based on metals and those that are not. Most minerals contain such metals as tin, copper, iron, and manganese, which are combined with other substances to form a chemical compound. Feldspar is made up of aluminum, potassium, sodium, and silica. Other minerals contain no metal, such as quartz and diamond.

A mineral deposit is found where any particular mineral has become concentrated. Mineral ores (concentrated deposits) are often mined and provide us with useful materials. There are many ways in which they might have become concentrated and it is not always possible for geologists to tell exactly how they came about.

It is thought that a large number of metal mineral deposits are found where there was once activity within the Earth's crust. For this reason they are often found with igneous rocks. One theory is that heat and water beneath the Earth's crust somehow dissolved the minerals from surrounding rocks. In this way they became concentrated. Minerals like this often have crystals that formed as the water cooled.

Many nonmetal mineral deposits, and some metal mineral deposits, exist as concentrated sediments. Usually it is easier for geologists to guess how these formed because the sedimentary processes (see page 36) are more obvious than the igneous processes (see page 28). They may have been redeposited from minerals washed out of rocks, like illite which is usually found in shale. Minerals more resistant to weathering, like quartz, may have been left behind as a deposit when their original rock was washed away. Other deposits may be completely original, like salt deposits. These were formed by sea water evaporation and are often called evaporites.

ACTIVITY

1 Look at your minerals through the magnifying glass. Can you see any straight-sided crystals?
2 Identify the minerals, using the book.
3 Are any of your minerals embedded in rock? If so, in what type of rock?
4 Go to a museum to see, and find out about, a wide range of minerals.

GEMSTONES

Gemstones are precious stones. They are precious because they are rare and beautiful. Diamond is probably the best-known gemstone. It is a crystal of pure carbon, which has been squashed under enormous pressure and heat. Diamond is the hardest natural substance.

There are many other gemstones, such as ruby, emerald, and sapphire. Gemstones are pure, or almost pure, mineral crystals. Tiny traces of other minerals give stones, such as ruby, their colors.

Diamonds are mined in parts of South Africa. They are formed deep in the Earth and under great pressure and heat, in a rock called kimberlite.

TEST YOURSELF

1. How are minerals grouped into two classes? Give examples of each class.
2. What are gemstones?
3. What is a diamond and how is it formed?

THE EFFECT OF PLANTS AND ANIMALS

Left Lichens and mosses grow well even without soil.

Below In tropical rain forests plants grow up and die off continually. The soil is protected by the cover of plants. If land is cleared for farming or grazing the soil is quickly eroded.

Small plants, such as lichens and mosses, can increase weathering by living in cracks in rocks. Their roots penetrate between the mineral grains that make up the rock, and split them apart. They also release acids that chemically weather minerals present in both rock and soil. These and other weathering processes, as well as deposition of eroded material, develop a soil that can support larger plants. As plants thrive, the organic content increases and the soil becomes deeper. This process continues until the largest plants that can grow in the local conditions are established.

All plants, especially trees, are good at preventing erosion of soil. Their roots help to keep the soil in place by acting like nets. Their branches and leaves decrease the impact of raindrops that would loosen small soil particles. The plant as a whole prevents water flowing away rapidly, eroding the soil with it. Larger plants act as windbreaks, cutting down the erosive power of the wind.

Animals and bacteria also change the soil in many ways. Earthworms, for example, transport soil from lower levels and deposit it on the surface. Their burrows allow water and air to circulate through the soil. Bacteria help the organic content to decay and increase humus in the soil.

ACTIVITY

YOU NEED

- **a small plastic aquarium tank**
- **soil**
- **peat**
- **6 live earthworms**
- **cellophane tape**
- **black paper**

1 Put the soil in the tank.
2 Put a layer of peat on the surface.
3 Place the earthworms in the peat.
4 To keep out the light, tape black paper to the sides of the tank.

5 Look at your earthworms each day in dim light. What are they doing to the soil and the peat?
6 Remember to keep the soil moist.

7 Please return the earthworms to their natural habitat.

An earthworm helps to improve soil by mixing it and breaking it up as it burrows and eats.

TEST YOURSELF

1. Explain how plants can weather rock.
2. Describe how plants protect soil.

AGRICULTURE AND SOIL

Plant cultivation by farmers affects the soil. Plowing, harrowing, and rolling can break down the soil structure. This means that the forces that stick soil together are destroyed. If the land is overcultivated, the fine soil particles can easily be blown or washed away. This happens especially if the land is left without plants or if fields are large and open.

The use of heavy machines on wet clay soils presses the soil into a dense, horizontal layer. This increases runoff (water flowing off the land) and therefore erosion. Plant growth is also reduced.

Cutting down trees to make more land for agriculture increases erosion (see page 42). Farmers can help to reduce erosion by planting windbreaks and hedges, or by building terraces on sloping ground.

Farmers alter soil by adding chemicals to it. Plants need nitrates (see page 14) to make protein. Crop yields are increased by adding nitrates and other artificial fertilizers to the soil. Rainwater dissolves some of these chemicals. The chemicals can reach our drinking water and can also affect plant and animal life in rivers and streams. Farmers also use poisonous chemicals as sprays to control plant diseases and pests. These pesticides also pollute the soil and groundwater. Some farmers are trying to protect the soil, humans, animals, and plants by organic farming. They use natural methods (no pesticides or artificial fertilizers) to grow crops.

Top right *Plowing is necessary for cultivation, but hedges and windbreaks can reduce the risk of soil being eroded.*

Right *Terraces and ridges like these at Pokhara, Nepal, can help prevent soil from being washed away in heavy rainfall.*

ACTIVITIES

LIME AND SOIL

YOU NEED

- **clay soil**
- **a spoon**
- **two jars**
- **a small bag of lime**

1 Remove the stones from the clay.
2 Put a spoonful of clay in both jars.

3 Fill the jars with water and shake them. What happens?
4 Add a spoonful of lime to one jar. Shake both jars again.

5 Allow both jars to stand.
6 Notice that the water in the jar with the lime is clearer. Lime has made the clay particles stick together, become heavier, and sink.
7 Farmers spread lime, which is alkaline, on their fields because it removes the acidity of the soil. Test the acidity of the water in each jar.

CONSERVATION AND AGRICULTURE

1 Visit your local garden shop. What fertilizers are sold?
2 How many pesticides and fungicides are for sale?
3 Read warning labels on the bags. How safe are these chemicals?
4 Contact your local conservation organizations. Is your groundwater polluted by farming chemicals? What is being done to stop this? Write a report of your findings.

TEST YOURSELF

1. What does plowing do to the soil?
2. What problems occur when farmers use heavy machinery on wet clay soil?
3. Describe how groundwater could become polluted.

Glossary

Atmosphere   The air around the Earth.

Bacteria   Tiny, one-celled organisms. Some live off plant and animal material and can cause its decay.

Bedrock   The solid rock underneath soil. Also called "parent rock" if it has broken up to form the soil above it.

Chemical weathering   The chemical reactions that break down rock.

Conglomerate   A sedimentary rock made of pebbles set in a finer material.

Continental drift   The theory that states that continents move on plates. Also called plate tectonics.

Convection currents   Circular (up-down) movements of liquids or gases caused by heat rising.

Cultivation   Farming of crops and plants.

Dinosaurs   Extinct reptiles that died out at the end of the Mesozoic era.

Eras   The largest time periods that divide the Earth's history.

Erosion   The processes by which forces, usually wind, water, and ice, wear down and carry away the surface of the land.

Extrusive rock   An igneous rock that has solidified from molten material on the Earth's surface.

Fault   A break or crack in the Earth's crust where the rocks move alongside each other.

Feldspar   A group of minerals that are found mostly in igneous rocks.

Fertilizers   Natural or artificial substances added to the soil in order to improve plant growth.

Fungicide   A chemical that kills fungi.

Geologist   A scientist who studies the structure of the Earth and its history.

Gravity   The force that pulls everything toward the center of the Earth.

Ice ages   Periods in the Earth's history that were colder than today. Ice sheets spread over areas that now have no ice.

Inorganic   Nonliving substances. This does not include material that was once living.

Intrusive rock   An igneous rock that has solidified below the Earth's surface.

Joints   Large cracks in a rock's structure made as the lava cools.

Legumes   Vegetables and plants that have root nodules containing bacteria that change nitrogen gas into a form usable by the plant.

Mechanical weathering   The breaking down of rocks by the action of wind, water, ice, and temperature changes.

Meteor   A piece of rock from space that burns up when it enters the Earth's atmosphere.

Meteorite   A meteor that reaches the surface of the Earth.

Methane   A natural fuel gas, produced from the decay of materials containing hydrogen and carbon, such as oil.

Minerals   Naturally occurring deposits of inorganic substances.

Nutrients   Materials needed for plant growth.

Obsidian   A glasslike igneous rock.

Organic   Living or once-living substances. Organic chemicals are based on carbon.

Pesticide   A chemical that destroys pests.

pH   The scale that describes how acidic or alkaline a substance is. A pH below 7 is acidic; a pH above 7 is alkaline; pH7 is neutral.

Plates Sections of the Earth's crust. Plates move due to hot currents in the mantle that push magma to the surface.

Pollution The release of substances that spoil the environment.

Protein The "building blocks" of living organisms. Skin and hair are examples of proteins. Plants make proteins, too.

Quartz A hard rock crystal found especially in sand and granite.

Reptiles A class of animals that are cold-blooded, such as snakes and lizards.

Richter scale The scale that expresses the intensity of an earthquake.

Scree Loose, weathered rock fragments that have rolled off a cliff or hill.

Solar system The sun and the planets that revolve around it.

Subduction zone An area where part of the Earth's crust is pushed down into the mantle.

Subsoil The layer of soil between the surface layer and the bedrock.

Topsoil The top layer of soil, usually containing organic material.

Tropics Very hot regions of the Earth, near the equator.

Weeds Plants that are growing where they are not wanted.

Books to Read

Earthquake, Brian Knapp (Steck-Vaughn, 1989)

Glacier, Ronald Bailey (Time-Life, 1982)

Mountains, Donna Bailey (Steck-Vaughn, 1990)

Mountains, Keith Lye (Silver Burdett, 1987)

Rivers and Lakes, Ronald Bailey (Time-Life, 1984)

Rocks and Minerals, Natural History Museum Staff (Knopf, 1988)

Spread of Deserts, Ewan McLeish (Steck-Vaughn, 1990)

Volcano, Brian Knapp (Steck-Vaughn, 1989)

Picture Acknowledgments

The author and publishers would like to thank the following for allowing the illustrations to be reproduced in this book: Geoscience Features Picture Library, 12 (left), 22, 23, 29, 34 (left), 44 (below); Jimmy Holmes, 25; Oxford Scientific Films, *cover* (below), 8, 10, 14, 24, 40, 42 (below), 43; Science Photo Library, 27, 33, 36; Topham Picture Library, 28, 32, 38, 39, 44 (above); Wayland Picture Library, *cover* (above), *frontispiece*, 6, 16 (left), 17, 30, 34 (below); ZEFA, 12 (below), 16 (right), 19, 26, 41, 42 (left). All artwork is by Marilyn Clay.

Index

DISCARDED.